Mary Engelbreit's
SUMMER

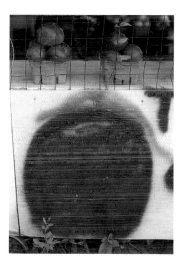

Mary Engelbreit's
SUMMER
CRAFT BOOK

Illustrated by Mary Engelbreit
Written by Charlotte Lyons
Photography by Barbara Elliott Martin

ANDREWS AND MCMEEL
A Universal Press Syndicate Company
Kansas City

is a registered trademark of Mary Engelbreit Enterprises, Inc.

10 9 8 7 6 5 4 3 2 1

Use of the Girl Scout name by permission of Girl Scouts® of the USA.

Library of Congress Cataloging-in-Publication Data

Engelbreit, Mary.
　　Mary Engelbreit's summer craft book / illustrated by Mary Engelbreit ; written by Charlotte Lyons ; photography by Barbara Elliott Martin.
　　　p.　cm.
　　ISBN 0-8362-2768-9 (hd)
　　1. Handicraft. 2. Summer. I. Lyons, Charlotte. II. Title.
TT157.E53　1997
745.5--dc20　　　　　　　　　　　　　　96-34006
　　　　　　　　　　　　　　　　　　　　CIP

Design by Stephanie Raaf

ATTENTION: SCHOOLS AND BUSINESSES
Andrews and McMeel books are available at quantity discounts with bulk purchase for educational, business, or sales promotional use. For information, please write to: Special Sales Department, Andrews and McMeel, 4520 Main Street, Kansas City, Missouri 64111.

Contents

one.
MEMORIAL
DAY

Wreath of Honor

Although the pool may officially open on Memorial Day, this is a holiday in honor of the men and women who have fought for our country's freedom. Celebrate their memory with this patriotic wreath.

Choose a sturdy willow or grapevine wreath and decorate it with a basket of trimmings from the craft store. The red, white, and blue ribbon weaves in and out among silk flowers and hot-glued charms. This would be a great project to do with children whose questions and curiosity will prompt stories about your family's special heroes.

memorial day

Flag Tray

Have some fun dressing up a serving tray with stars and stripes.

Paint the inner and outer rim and the underside of an unfinished wooden tray royal blue and paper the inside with a road map or some other interesting paper. In the upper left hand corner, outline a rectangle and paint it with a watercolor wash, let dry and glue on assorted buttons for stars and then scraps of rickrack for stripes. Seal and protect with a pour-on resin sealer or a piece of glass cut to size. To finish, decorate the outside edge with dimensional or handpainted lettering and, if you like, add a faux flagpole made from a wooden dowel or small flag holder.

Rice Salad

*This do-ahead rice salad adds spirited color
and taste to the holiday picnic table.*

Have ready 3 cups of chilled cooked rice. (For added flavor, cook the rice in chicken broth with a pressed clove of garlic.) In a large bowl, mix the rice with 1/2 cup chopped black olives, 1/2 cup chopped red pepper, and 3 or 4 chopped scallions. Add 1/8 cup chopped fresh basil, 1/8 cup chopped fresh parsley, 6 tablespoons olive oil, 2 tablespoons wine vinegar, and freshly ground pepper and salt to taste. Toss lightly and chill several hours before serving. Serves 4–6.

memorial day

SO MUCH OF WHAT WE KNOW OF LOVE WE LEARN · AT · HOME

two.
FATHER'S
DAY

Bookend Frame

*Use some of your time and talents to make
a gift for Dad that he will cherish.
This trophy picture frame
does double-duty as a bookend.*

egin with a crafter's plaque as a base. Mix and
match wooden letters and shapes into a sculp-
ture that spells Dad. The D will be the frame opening. When you have all the materials assembled, use
acrylic paints to paint them in the colors of your
choice and seal them with an acrylic sealer to give
a smooth, finished look. Use the D as a pattern and
cut one of acetate and another of cardboard to use
for the frame. Assemble the painted D, acetate,
photo, and cardboard to make a frame. Add extra
decorations such as rickrack and charms, then glue
all the elements together.

Papier-mâché
Desk Set

*Dad will never believe you made this from
a juice can and a cracker box!*

Cut the top of the can into a wavy rim. Draw the pattern of house and trees onto the back of the empty box. Cut around it with the scissors to create the silhouette and cut the remaining three sides down to about 3 inches high. Mix papier-mâché paste (1 cup water, 1/2 cup flour, 1 tablespoon glue) and tear newspaper into strips. Dip the strips into the paste and layer onto the box to strengthen and build up the sides and back. Paint the juice can while you wait for the box to dry. When dry, paint the box white and then in the colors of your choice. Seal with an acrylic sealer inside and out. To finish, glue chunky wooden beads on the bottom of each piece for feet.

father's day

Tackle Box

*Maybe this project will even inspire
a riverside day trip.*

S pray-paint a tool or tackle box and then make it a one-of-a-kind carryall with wooden cutouts, letters, beads, and other accents of your choice. Plastic ferns and glass baubles for bubbles give an underwater look to this one, but anything goes if your imagination comes up with another approach. Don't forget to fill the inside with fishing hooks, lures, and directions to a favorite fishing hole.

father's day

three.
SUMMER
BACKYARD

Seed Box

Spring planting is long over, but those seed packets are still important references. Store them in a distinctive box.

ny old box will do as long as it is sturdy. Decorate the sides and top edges with interesting paper, ribbons, or rickrack. Then focus on the top. This one features a copy of an old print found at a flea market. It is decoupaged onto the top along with cutout pictures of blossoms. Simply paste these on with thinned white glue or wallpaper paste. Leaves cut from a decorative paper unify the look and the twig frame adds an extra effect. A little notebook tucked inside is useful as a record of your plant discoveries this summer. It will be invaluable next spring when you choose your favorites again.

summer backyard

Plant Stakes

*Brighten your green garden
with these plant stakes that guide the hose,
line the path, or mark the rows.*

Make patterns for your favorite garden images and then transfer them to a 3/4-inch pine board. Cut out the shape with a jigsaw and then drill a hole in the bottom edge to fit a dowel that is cut to a length of 36 inches or more. Lightly sand any rough edges. Paint the shapes and the dowels, too. Seal with several coats of acrylic sealer so that they are weather-resistant. Attach your cutouts to the dowels with a little glue at the joint. To avoid stressing the dowel, use a spare dowel or pipe to poke a hole in the ground before installing the plant stakes in the garden.

Porch Pillows

*Cozy up the porch
with these quick and easy pillows
that you can make while the sun tea brews.*

tore-bought striped pillows take on plenty
of personality with a little extra trim and
time. Simply sew on a cluster of cherry red
buttons and a stem tweaked off a silk flower
stalk. A few stitches with embroidery floss make
it come together securely. Around the edges, a
length or two of rickrack or fringe frames each
one with bright summery colors.

Patio Lantern

*Lingering outdoors beneath the stars
is one of the pleasures of summer.
Build this starry teapot lantern for your garden
patio and enjoy those evenings outside.*

ind an old metal teapot or coffeepot from the thrift shop or a garage sale. Use a drill fitted with a metal bit to drill holes randomly all over it for a lantern effect. Paint the lid and handle with acrylic enamels. Illuminate with a small candle that won't create too much heat. Be cautious of the hot metal sides. Better yet, use a small flashlight.

Window Dressing

*While you have the paints out, treat
your window boxes to a painted-on petticoat.*

egin with a fresh coat of paint as a base. If your
window box already has a fancy apron, great! If
it doesn't, you can paint one on with swags and blossoms like these. After penciling on a design, go over
it with paint colors that harmonize with your house
colors and the plants you intend to put in the box.
Finish your work with an acrylic sealer, hang, and
plant with your favorite combination of blooms.

Truck Garden

*Romance a summer table with flea market
finds and garden picks.*

This well-loved toy truck still comes out to play,
but this time it carries a load of cobalt blue bot-
tles as bud vases. A handful of cut flowers and a
sunny bowl of tomatoes bring fragrance and color
to a cool porch corner. Even the table takes on new
charm with a fresh mosaic of broken blue and white
dishes. Use your lazy summer days and unstoppable
ingenuity to make the most of what you already have
and especially love.

summer backyard

Gazpacho

Ask a friend for lunch, set a pretty table,
and enjoy this simple, refreshing cold soup
that makes the most of the garden.

hop 6 tomatoes, 2 cucumbers, 1 green pepper, and 1 onion. Place in a large bowl. Add 1 or 2 cloves minced garlic, 1 grated carrot (optional), several tablespoons each chopped fresh parsley, basil, 2 cups tomato juice, 1/4 cup olive oil, 2 or 3 tablespoons wine vinegar, and the juice of half a lemon. Adjust to taste with more vinegar or tomato juice, salt, and pepper. If you prefer a smoother texture, puree in the blender briefly. Chill at least 4 hours. Serve in chilled bowls with one or two of the following as a garnish: croutons, grated carrots, chopped herbs, or lemon slices. Serves 4-6.

summer backyard

four.
FOURTH OF JULY

Parade Hat

They'll have no trouble finding you in a crowd,
and you'll be shaded and cool
beneath this festive sun hat.

A store-bought straw hat takes white acrylic paint for stenciled polka dots and freehand water waves as a border. A short length of gingham ribbon meets at the back with a bow fashioned from a parade flag pinched in the center. Stitch it in place and top with a shiny brass button.

fourth of july

Best-of-Show Bike

*Organize a neighborhood bike parade and
inspire the block with this grand-prize entry.*

If you have an old bike in the back of the garage,
now is the time to clean it up and decorate it with
sparkle and charm. A thrift shop basket spray-
painted red and filled with straw and sunflowers
sits snugly against handlebars wrapped in ribbons
and spangled trim. Quick changes like the gingham-
wrapped seat and woven wheel spokes are easy to
do. This is one time when you need not worry about
overdoing it—as long as you can still ride the bike.
Then again, it looks mighty cute just parked at the
gate in front of your house.

Folk Art Flag

Put the kids to work on this funky flag project.
It will be the picnic showstopper!

A bag of landscaping rocks from the garden center did the trick for this backyard garden flag. After washing them and laying each rock out in formation to dry, paint them one at a time with glossy acrylic enamels. Add a few stars here and there and that's it. Hint: if you choose a grassy stage, be sure you mow it first!

Blueberry Muffins

*In the morning—before the kitchen heats up—
bake these quick muffins for breakfast.*

The trick to light, delicious muffins is quick mixing. Preheat the oven to 400 degrees. In a large bowl combine 1 3/4 cups flour, 1/4 cup sugar, 2 1/2 teaspoons baking powder, and 1/2 teaspoon salt. In a separate bowl, whisk 1 egg with 3/4 cup milk and 1/3 cup vegetable oil. Add this to the dry ingredients and stir briefly only until mixed. Fold in 1 to 1 1/2 cups fresh blueberries. Fill greased muffin cups 3/4 full and bake for 20 minutes until golden brown. This recipe makes one dozen muffins.

five.
SUMMER
CAMP

Painted Trunk

Send your youngster off in style
with this painted camp trunk.

Scout around at flea markets, church sales, and thrift stores for an old trunk that strikes your fancy. Give it a fresh base coat of paint and then decorate it with acrylic paints to spark it up. Maybe you'll want to decoupage it instead—consider road maps, Scout manuals, or nature cutouts. Or hand the project over to your camper and let him do his own thing. Be sure to seal the finished work with an acrylic sealer that will protect everything from the bumps and bruises of travel.

summer camp

Laundry Bag

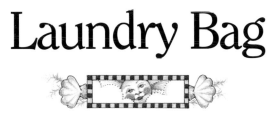

Hopefully, this eye-catching laundry bag might catch the dirty clothes, too. It's a start.

Begin with a purchased pillowcase or sew up one of your own. Make a big side pocket with a no-sew fusible fabric flower like this one or choose your own design. Stitch the pocket onto the bag along with a colorful casing strip near the top. Finish with a ribbon drawstring. For the bus ride, stick your camper's pillow inside and slip a good book or two in the pocket.

Letter Case

Make letters home a priority with this letter case made from an old blue jean leg.

Open up the leg of blue-jean cutoffs so that the seams are in the position shown here. Cut a rectangle 18 inches high by 12 inches wide. Use the factory hem as the top edge. Cut a rectangle of lining fabric to match, but add a 1/2 inch seam allowance to the top. Right sides together, sew along three sides leaving the top (the factory hem) open. Turn right side out and press. Fold the lining seam allowance under and blindstitch. Fold the bottom up 6 inches, pin, and topstitch along the sides. Fold the top down and sew two snaps into place for closure. Decorate the front with felt cut-outs. Fill with cards and stationery prestamped and addressed home.

Care Package

*There's nothing like a box of goodies from home.
This one will be the envy of everyone
in the cabin.*

Use brown craft paper, colored markers and pencils to turn an ordinary box into a sentimental wonder. A garden of flowers, a family pet, and a secret message find spots here and there against a house that could be home. Be sure to reserve a place for a clear mailing label on top. Handle with care!

Rustic Frame

*In your care package, send this frame you can
make from backyard twigs.*

First, cut three twigs from a shrub or tree that
make a triangle shape and two small pieces for
a stand. Cut a mat board backing to fit and cut a
photo opening from the inside. Hot-glue the three
larger twigs together and set aside. Decorate the
mat board opening with a strip of leather woven
through punched holes (use an awl for this). Add
rickrack trims and ornaments wherever desired.
Assemble the twig frame with the mat board backing using a glue gun and continue to decorate as
needed. Attach a photograph to the back and another backing of cardboard. Glue the two remaining
small twigs perpendicular to the base for a stand.

Bunkmate Organizer

Cabin living is cozy with limited personal space.
This organizer keeps everything right at hand
in close quarters.

Another way to use old blue jeans! Cut the back off and stitch to a bigger envelope of fabric. (Make this to fit a piece of foam core that slips inside and adds stability.) This makes a big pocket out of the seat and lets you use the little pockets for whatever else. The foam core inside acts like a bulletin board for extra pinups. Hang from three ribbon ties on the wall and fill it with fun stuff to do and snapshots from home.

summer camp

Autograph Pillow

*Camp friends are hard to leave behind.
Make this sweet pillow from an old T-shirt
so that everyone can autograph it
with personality and fondness.*

Choose the best part of a clean shirt with the camp logo centered. Cut a rectangle for the pillow front with seam allowance all around. From the back of the shirt, cut a matching rectangle for the back of the pillow. Construct the pillow with cording and a contrasting double ruffle, if you wish. Turn and fill with fiberfill stuffing. Close opening. Send the pillow along with a set of permanent or fabric markers. Let the fun begin!

summer camp

six.
VACATION

Beach Bag

*A straw bag especially for the beach
keeps everything in one spot and is ready
to go in a grab.*

Transform a store-bought bag with fabric strips torn from extra yard goods. Weave them in and out of the bag openings rag-rug style. Tuck the raw ends into the bag at the sides and then fluff up the strips on the outside. Consider adding a big decoration like this flower made from a straw drink coaster and scraps of felt. Big basting stitches hold it in place. In fact, take the whole project to the beach and make it while the kids build a castle. You'll be finished first.

vacation

Sand Throne

*Stake your spot in the sand
with this cute painted chair and banners.*

Fancy lettering with acrylic paint turns this canvas sand chair into a personal throne. Pencil your design and then paint over it with a good brush and two coats where needed. While you're at it, make these sand banners so that the kids can find you at the crowded beach when they return from playing nearby. Felt panels hanging from dowels are enhanced with more felt designs cut and glued onto the banners. Staked in the sand, they mark your spot.

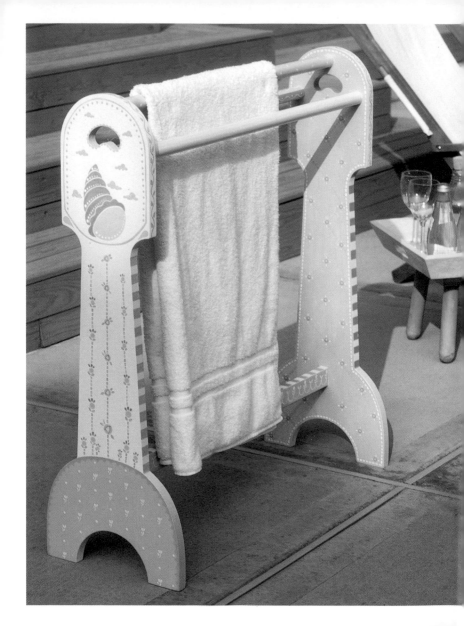

Towel Rack

*Mix-and-match patterns and colors
enhance this towel rack.*

Indoors or out, this practical accessory lends charm and loveliness with soft, muted colors and small print patterns. Decorated with a limited palette of acrylic paints over a base coat, the design makes the most of edges and small areas. Repeat patterns are a good way to fill larger areas. Once again, don't forget to seal the work with an acrylic sealer for protection against moisture.

Beach Towel

*Add bright trimmings and pockets to a plain
beach towel for seaside comfort.*

A few vintage luncheon napkins were just the
right size for pockets on this oversized, fluffy
beach towel. Each one holds a magazine or sun-
glasses and keeps them near at hand and free from
sand. Sew the napkins on with rickrack trim and
add a zesty border of fringed ribbon along the towel
edges for more decoration.

Lemonade Pitcher

Lemonade looks much cooler in this sweetly painted pitcher.

Spend a summer day at home with your imagination and paints, and a plain glass pitcher. Use glossy acrylic enamels that can be heat-set in the oven for added permanence. Some areas can be sponged on rather than brushed for a different effect. Even the handle is transformed into a Loch Ness water beast. Paint one as a hostess gift for your friend with a cottage at the beach. She'll invite you again next year.

Sailing Shelf

*A seaside collection
calls for a special showcase.*

Build this corner sailboat shelf based on a vintage flea market find. Sketch out a sailing ship silhouette on newspaper and fold the newspaper in half. Cut the paper at the fold and use each side for a pattern. Use 1/4 inch luan plywood and cut out the two sides allowing for extra material at the joint. A jigsaw works best and will cut out the interior shapes if you drill a hole first. Then make patterns for shelves and cut them out. Glue and nail the pieces together. Paint and hang.

Contributors

Project Designs

Mary Engelbreit: Window Dressing, Patio Lantern, Sailing Shelf

Charlotte Lyons: Rice Salad, Papier-mâché Desk Set, Seed Box, Truck Garden, Gazpacho, Parade Hat, Folk Art Flag, Blueberry Muffins, Laundry Bag, Letter Case, Bunkmate Organizer, Autograph Pillow, Beach Bag, Beach Towel

Michael Mahler for Cheap Trx: Painted Trunk

Joseph Slattery: Wreath of Honor, Flag Tray, Bookend Frame, Tackle Box, Plant Stakes, Porch Pillows, Best-of-Show Bike, Care Package, Rustic Frame, Sand Throne, Lemonade Pitcher

Stephanie Barken: Towel Rack

Grateful Appreciation to

Girl Scouts of America
Betsy Holowaluk
Schoene Kurlbaum
New Piasa Chautauqua, Illinois
Steven and Susan Smith
Sonja and Bob Willman
Andy Wiltse
Michael Dinges and Robin Winge
Jean Lowe, Stephanie Raaf, Stephanie Barken,
and Dave Bari

Index